RIVER OF YOUR DAYS

Elizabeth Carriere

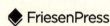

FriesenPress

One Printers Way
Altona, MB R0G 0B0
Canada

www.friesenpress.com

Copyright © 2023 by **Elizabeth Carriere**
First Edition — 2023

All rights reserved.

No part of this publication may be reproduced in any form, or by any means, electronic or mechanical, including photocopying, recording, or any information browsing, storage, or retrieval system, without permission in writing from FriesenPress.

ISBN
978-1-03-916284-6 (Hardcover)
978-1-03-916283-9 (Paperback)
978-1-03-916285-3 (eBook)

1. Poetry, Subjects & Themes, Nature

Distributed to the trade by The Ingram Book Company

*For my mother
who taught me to wonder, and to love*

How dear to her is the journey of the mind,
Flying from dwelling to dwelling,
—Anne Szumigalski
FROM *On Glassy Wings*

TABLE OF CONTENTS

Snow Water Light   *1*

Africa   *23*

War and Beauty   *33*

Leaving   *51*

About the author   *71*

SNOW WATER LIGHT

River of Your Days

When what is unbearable
    speaks to us
When the hummingbird
    keeps its distance
When you glimpse the outline
    of the willow
When the bamboo still bends
    under snow
When on the screen there is fire
    and resistance
A woman and her child
    sleep perhaps
Their bodies lie against
    the broken steps
When the forsythia
    releases its buds
Into a small economy
    of yellow blossoms
When all you have
    is packed in this small box
When you gently rock
    to a strain of music
When you hear a thrush whistle
    under the dying hemlock
And a lone black fly strikes
    against the glass
When a friend makes a pattern like frost
    as she moves

ELIZABETH CARRIERE

When you walk up from the ocean
    holding a sprig of new green leaves
When water steams into fog
    that hangs below the snowline
When a man inhales
    and his face
Is hidden by smoke
    as he exhales
When you eat a pear imported
    from that country
Where girls
    are sold for bread
When the good earth
Drums its hollow sound
    in a sulcus of melting ice
And this becomes
    the river of your days

Snow

My eyes catch sight of snow knowing there is no snow
knowing I might have held snow
as I might have held the imprint of night

I think there is shadow that swallows all shadows

that moves from room to room
its sound is shapeless like cloth fallen from a body

Outside this room there is rain and there is mist
rain makes that *s* sound like jazz
at the horizon a wolf kills for pleasure
in the thin hour before twilight

Here now is my practice of being, I only want
the woods and the waiting
the nights are ravens wheeling in the sturdy dark

Your arrival must be a feather lighter than a tune

like yesterday but truer
a feather sleeping in the melting snow

ELIZABETH CARRIERE

Imagined letter from my child

I read through and through what you
wrote what you write what

you have not written.

It is a long story about
your body learning to love itself.

An elegant craft it moves through
water, it burns like a flood.

Sky sets in. A ribbon opens
the gift you are inside of, tied

to the river, lashed
to every season. I am listening

yet you move
with or without me.

I am sad with love. I tell you
your beauty is wondrous made

flesh as childhood
leaves its country of snow.

Finally here is the doe.
Alert, quiet like winter.

Meaning you see me looking
another way
through a different dark.

Crow

I am still here with the crow
caught in his nettle of black feathers

there at his neck, where a white tuft
like age appears below his right eye

this crow knows things
I keep him close

there is a promise written
by his feet folded round the wire

on which he rests
if he rests

he is noisy
holds on

or forgets
to let go

ELIZABETH CARRIERE

Gambier

Will I find the seasons
have proceeded without me?

I walk the graveled road.
Up the hill there's a corner
a narrow lane pungent
with cedar. It's my place
but it grows or dissembles
without me. Not this time.

I am a crowd arriving.
Come in you say or perhaps
you are not there at all.
The view is god the trampled
grass her angels.

House

The light undoes itself
from deepest grey
a flash catches the edge
of sight—a silver gull wheeling
endlessly in a dull sky

We wait—the ferry will arrive
knocking the water into a hungry surge
that could but doesn't eat
the small boats nesting at the pier

By now it's dusk and up at the house
we lounge in wait for night glasses filled
you give me news of a friend paralyzed
when his heart paused just those few seconds
the dog curls in sleep twitching
to music we argue over

Its good isn't it this life
bewitched between the hours
that pass as lines as notes
our heads warmed and nodding
by a tidy fire with all its craving

You stand away
watching the night do nothing
on the other side of the glass
you of all people know how the wild dark
sharpens against the stones just past
our narrow line of sight

ELIZABETH CARRIERE

I take your hand and walk you
into the cooling air the balm
of pine scent the birds settling in their
straw nets—noises of safety before
the day's last shadow grey green
and sensational shoots through
the trees' black line

Child

I write this backwards. Pull one end
as string through this story's throat.
I am surer of it now. What I am sent
to make, what I am sent to watch.

How evening drapes the light. The shapes
the sea deposits at its edges. The deep
significance of stupidity.

I say well here we are. Always
for the first time, no matter
how often. Your eyes blue as death.

Your words yesterday.
Doors closing. What
would have been a house with a child
with a mind of her own.

That child is not mine. She
is an alien child—mix of starfish and ash, small
cockle tossed on the ocean's froth. At least
that's how I remember her.

Time to come in, a mother's call. The garden
darkens. Birds make their clearing-up sound—
the whole day lodges in their throats.

Who does the day belong to? It is evening,
it does not matter. Or I don't know.
I don't know: What is it to know?

ELIZABETH CARRIERE

What Dreams

what dreams ride up like thunder
as unlimited air reaches its perimeter of blue

bird achieves an altitude
where heat crumples against a fist of hail

what is it we shout when this sky
is troubled not by light

but by the steady will of thunder
pushing the season to its horizon

elements answer thrashing
against the inevitable winter of words

a climate defeated by its own
dreadful act of snow

Mermaids

god sees me returning to a room filled
to its ceiling with sea. the sea churns
with chunks of ice and starfish. falling ships
stain the seabed with the colour of their descent.
bodies are mermaids swimming
their scaly faces roll upward to a far surface light.
oh I am here with all the dreamers.
we are happy, we are drowning in our beds.

ELIZABETH CARRIERE

Water

The way to December is steep.
Water with its litany of rushing
and ebbing has worn away
the green bloom on
the cliffs of each month.
In November maple trees
give up their great golden leaves.

Earlier a riot of violet irises
rose like spears from
a neighbour's black pond and summer
was strung like a flowered dress
so delicate the sun passed
through those places already worn.

I first came in the spring and walked
between the cedars and the streams.
Water pinned by barrettes
of weeds held back her prodigal hair and
all that laughter.

Now the ditches fill with thorns
and dead yellow grasses.
Water is an alchemy of sad things passing—
the fires the sawdust the stricken
fallen trees the drought the thirsty wells.
Then the rains
the rains.
And so many things slide away.

Yet here are these six ducks
crowned in their sheen
of green headfeathers
their emphatic fleshy feet
write in orange on the road they cross
we're here
we're here we're here.

ELIZABETH CARRIERE

Hummingbird's Heart

It quietens me
to hear you speak of the humming-
bird's heart how it shakes the world

You sketch the drift of late snow
on the still fragile ice
the lake at rest

You in the garden gentler
than even the fall of folded leaves

Your old eyes you say
cloud with longing
for a different kind of sight

Let me be with you that moment
you don't know me
and I no longer know me

We want the same thing
as all that is breathing turns away
in the quiet fashion
of the end of every summer

A Raven Stopped

Let us long for what never returns
the sparse remains of winter
that winter when what was in snow

could not last and could not be found
in the spring melt nor the songs of
birds rising from their season of silence

I want simplicity forced
upon me lack of things as I move
between this and that life

a beetle iridescent in its moment
crawls without regret between the sun
and another dark pod of earth

we need time but cannot rest
all that moves passes through us
without pausing but still we are changed

the speed of the fox its green
eye fixes you it travels into
and out of you like hope and envy

how I would be here with you
a raven stopped in midair
if it is not diving, falls

ELIZABETH CARRIERE

Moon

How are you with the moon
the night for instance how
do you manage the vastness
points of no return
vertigo at the locus
of sleep your arms around
nothing or waking
when it is still night
the moon a blind cat
at your window
your pillow full of snow

Journey with me this time
midnight
turns to grey ash
there are those who can't
return and those
who won't be warned
the bush becomes coal
singed beyond belief
red field of chronicles
earth crusting at will

How are you with this
the wild and the sweet
mixed as birdsong
when dawn takes you
bandaged in cloud mist
and sulfur still rises
and the earth remains a wound
is it enough that too much
dies and so much tries to die

Another Spring

I think I hear a flute but it is the raven
pacing the heavy sky. If it rains
we will know if it's spring or winter's worn closure.
I make a fire to burn deadfall
resurrected from a late brief snow,
wood faded to the hopeless white of bones.

I remember you as the ashes dim.
The very last thing I wanted
comes back in a later dream,
a foreign artefact this thing
that made us old in that one night.

In this moment let me do as I wish.
Is it waking for a moment
to feel the craft of a good day
still inventing itself.
I dress in the halflight,
the dark lounges in air thick with oxygen
and the spices of the sleeper's breathing.

ELIZABETH CARRIERE

Lake

A stone ripples the lake's skin. Rings of water
    hold like rope
the shape of a woman. Or at least
    the shape
of the stone thrown
    into an unformed place.

I do not speak of depth. It is
    unknown matter
arranged as fish weary from turning
    fresh water into air.
Their skin silver in a world that wants
    gold they are tapers lighting
a blurred tapestry of weeds. So much
    for the lake
and its gloomy edge where we have not
    yet travelled.

The lake is liquid set in a ring of clay. Shallow
    as pearls but clearer
holding above itself a dry firmament.
    A bowl
of dark problems hung with
    mollusk-shaped moons
rising.

Home

Sad matter of passion
falls like a silken scarf.
Sweet green rain
wishes itself against the leaves,
and light softens
at the field's edge.

Before nightfall
liquid birdsong pools.
What is called in, comes.
In the room's waiting
even the water's breath
is still.
The air is a voice
calling itself home.

AFRICA

Sahara Dust

There is no rest even for those
who pray. They come upon the colour

of rust in the place they kneel
expecting Lot's white salt

or stone the shade of ice.
It is the dawn wind

that pulls the earnest sparrow
through the bronze horizon.

Dry season.
Dust is what we see. Intimate

to us as our own innocent feet,
our skin made from sun.

Dust is earth bred with wind
laid along naked ground.

Limbs of flowers open and blur
confused by the suddenness

of evening, the
perpetual delay of light.

ELIZABETH CARRIERE

Thorn Bird Sees Us

The air is rich with detail
when thorn bird descends
in her web of oxygen
and settles herself into the early

day. She owns the view.
A lizard rubs away his disguise
against a black stone. Warthog
nuzzles the skin of grass

that clothes the dry
earth. If I look out over your
arm draped across my body
to the scrub bush (unwatered
patch of dust
that describes itself
as promise)
I see you as horizon.

Thorn bird sees the snake's
boneless movement
noosing its beauty
around a leafless branch.

Green scarf, your shoulder,
the whole of Africa
between us.

Rwanda

We've had our rain. Enough has been said.
Black clods crumble before they are drenched.
The creek tires of its own dry stones.

A small boy plays. His hands liquid in the water.
Something transparent dissolves to a silver wish.
He has time. Dark stretches beyond the red horizon.
Nightbirds clothe themselves in the evening hush.

A man opens the door upon his patch of earth
comforted by what he believes is his.
He claims the blue-tinged voice of the nightingale
the red ant ploughing its private way
toward its own eternity in borrowed ground.
The mountain's ashy smoke rises beyond green hills.
He owns all of this.

He sees over there trees fruiting on the shoulder
of the mountain. Green flags for a country still rising.
There is singing not for joy but remembrance.
He will know that the earth holds salt from ashes,
when the land lightens to grey.

That thing a man does with music whose universe
is his small green yard. It rises
like a concerto for single instrument.
Footfall of the brown-faced mouse
tap tap
against the hollow body of the night.

ELIZABETH CARRIERE

Immaculée

She pushes small sticks
into the three-stone fire
under a pot of red beans
that will cook all afternoon
for a single meal at dusk.

We have spoons and soap
today and the shy language
of the two-year-old
who is learning on her own
to sit on a small bench
and wait her turn.

Lost (South Sudan)

    they
were burned in the fire
    that burned their farms but

    they
survived

    they
stole clothes from the dead

    some of them were men
most were boys

the women had gone ahead
    they
were lost with their children

the boys and men were
    damaged and
    they
were lost

fire and dust burned their feet
    they
walked west

some walked east
    they
were lost

    they
walked for months until
    they
were found

ELIZABETH CARRIERE

    famished and crazed
outside the ring of tents

    inside there was water
and more people whose eyes
    burned with loss

    they
waited in the camps
    it could have been years

some left the tents
    they
walked and died

there was no water and
    then there was too much water

the Nile ate the dead
    and washed the living

    they
came to our door
    but we had left
because of the danger
    weary
    they
slept on the bare floor

we heard
    that soldiers took
    them
in the morning

Goma

Three colours of plastic slippers
from China lined
against black volcanic stones
for your feet try them
perfect as the slivers of fruit
on a flowered tin plate
sudden orange scent
for this girl with dirt in her
tightly braided green hair

Four pieces of African cloth
funnel their patterns
intricate as snakes
twisted headscarf
opulent print tight
against that woman's grace

Five times is enough
to say no to the boy
who wants to carry your bag
says *give me money*
looks at your face your shoes
counts what you know
you owe him

You hold six coins
drop them one by one
in the red plastic dish
of the blind man
at the hotel gate he
says *that last one foreign*

WAR AND BEAUTY

Five Wars

1.

Bored by beauty
the snake moves past the green
frog concealed in the grass as a drop of rain

The day's rain clings to the forest like crystal

There are bits of splintered glass
among red discs of petals in a flower bed

Between broken bricks the spider labours in the rich tannin
if there were still a pond there would be bright yellow fish

What do your eyes see but the sap bleeding from the trunk
the white froth on the twig marking the worm's route to its destiny

You stand in the garden that grows inside you
the sinking trees talk softly amongst themselves

The sun sets like quartz above a small boat stalled in the bay

The sky grows grey after its brief glory
it is late: your body disappears into the setting earth

The night webs its dark across your face
like a friend who knows what's best for you

2.

A bird of prey rises in the spring updraft
drops a stolen ring of flesh into the parched undergrowth

Unexpectedly I remember the dead
or I remember death

Under the upward branches of the hemlock
the dry brown brush descends
geometric and desiccated

In the city the lost die like old trees

You walk into the forest eyes closed hands extended
moss peels from the stones in the heat

Trees fall around all you, burning
there is no excuse for this

3.

In spring geraniums bloom red against green-black leaves
a rabbit stops on the stone path

Soon apple blossoms will open
against branches still charred from winter

What do we dream? the liquid of our thoughts
drowns us but we always survive

We arrive on time and nothing leaves without us
as if we deserve this

The world waits and smoulders
they say there will be blood

Shots in the night and we
in our bedclothes crouch somewhere in our paper house

4.

A night owl hunts in the shadows
just beyond the window of the guest room

A tree's round leaves blur the aura
of the last surge of light

The armed man who guards the dark sings softly to himself
he crouches near the gate smoking

We are both awake the night air enters the window
like water like indigo

I wait for it
the sudden curse of red lava
the warm snake marvelling along the marble tile
marking its calligraphy in the kitchen

Under cover of darkness are the first words
of the book I put down before sleeping

5.

What resembles silver
more than the desire for silver

A child is delighted on hearing the spring thrush
on finding a sole marigold missed by the late frost

Pausing on a bridge of stone a snake warms itself
its skin hardens to a shine before it peels away

Your lover is clothed she is unclothed
she will wear the bracelets you gave her

A child remains unborn
lost in the liquid of her mother's death

In a cold kitchen beneath a wooden table
a woman lies under her crumpled coat

A soldier holds what he has found on her wrist
a silver ring that says *To All Our Tomorrows*

The soldier crouches behind the metal of his weapon
later he is shot near the road by his companions

What she said to her lover

Look at my face.
Yes I am asking,
look at the bruised
imprint above my lip. There.
Like a kiss, a moustache,
a shadow,
a brushing past of something.
No it is not your fault. What
has fallen fell. Those
ungiven things. Those
moments after dusk.
All the unbreathing, so much
hunger and regret. Look again
these are my hands,
incidental in this hand—
holding and the reaching
that goes on nonetheless. Part
digit part heart—unreadable.

ELIZABETH CARRIERE

Predator

I suppose he pauses where I pause.
Needs the water between stones
like me. Needs this soft place
where reeds knit together
to rest. The smell of bloodless earth.
Sudden buds of berry flowers
crouched close on the ground
crushed against the creek's stone borders.
Froth gathers in crevices like soap.

And especially he needs the
withdrawal of light. A single
dark where now he can see.
And I am blind except my skin.

Earthquake

I ran out to the garden
    it was shaking
its gentleness surprised me
    bricks and walls graceful
in their curved collapse

We quarreled it was graceful too
    the toppling
architecture what flesh
    had built exposed
as ruin the tattered sleeve
    of your attention
barely covering
    the throbbing wrist

When it was gone the bluest
    dawn came back an eye
opened like a star
    what was bought with
that small coin of pain
    picked clean, the latticed bone
of the dead bird's wing
    nested in the ruin
crushed in its last charge
    against the shaking glass

ELIZABETH CARRIERE

Radiant

A drop of water hangs on the lip
of a copper cup

A star travels upward to the heart
of a dying woman

Flames eat at the base
of a parched hemlock

Old people sleep crumpled
on a winter street

A child listens head tilted
to a tune hummed by his mother

You scramble through a dream
along a path that opens as it follows you

Again and again
sleep reaches for you

In the morning you will climb through snow
to a house small as a bright jewel

Inside a fire is lit you drink
buttered tea from a china cup

A field spreads below you
pink thistle blooms spines soft as fur

You see the birds:

A gull mourning its mate
settles on a dry crust

A finch struggles to unlock
a hard pod of seeds

Your love fights a faraway
war lies down in a field
his body opens releases
sweet flowers grey metal

There is sunshine in a distant city
couples meet at the roundabout

Dressed for their wedding pictures
they are radiant

ELIZABETH CARRIERE

Beauty

I tried to read
but could not read.
Was it my eyes today?
Meaning was everywhere
and I was blind.

Quiet came that way.
Through touch I found your face
long after you had left the room.
Poet says:
Bird says:
I am listening.

And now beauty is told
as a small child's boots
left by the back step.
As a frog under his leaf.
Night.
First words.
A thread. No more
than that. Suspense.

Here

I am lost in all these countries
in hearts and blue nights
in tiny churches hallowed
by wind

In washed-up rubbish at the shore's edge
seabirds fight
their wings caked with muck and oil

How pale the moon
pulled into the scattered stars that mark these
coordinates of abundance

I am lost in an imagined space
written into mystery a place no poem
will go

I am here on my knees again
touching the snow the warren
of melt where the deer mouse
laid her pups

Last fever of winter
a woman laughing
in the dark lit
only by that sound

ELIZABETH CARRIERE

Your Hand

It is soft the way
the light like wind
lifts the edges of solid things

As though our parents were
here again wanting to explain
everything to us despite
the dark despite the sun
chiselling at the day

It is like camping the stars
in charge of time
the border with midnight
a creature we must
come to understand

I come back to softness
there is so much of
it from a distance
it might be grass or hair
or flame on a branch

And in that moment I
walk on turn my head
away from a field of
people sleeping or dead

If I had your hand now
how strong would I be
would I open the field
with all its fire and bones
and simply listen to
truth in human
stillness or truth
in the great noise
of all those bodies
breathing in

ELIZABETH CARRIERE

Walking

I'm out there walking
where the prairie pushes
its white horizon into an even whiter sky
I'll be walking with my father
who I am learning to forgive
in his eastern winter
in his eastern war

Out there soldiers' feet freeze in the boots
of their dead brothers
they walk for weeks fall like dark clots
on the trackless snow
I will be out there gathering
them death by death

I cannot hold them they are not
meant to be held
my arms overflow with garlands
the creamy shade of bones

You worry at my distance but you do not call me back.
I am in a helicopter rising from a place of false refuge.
I am washed in rivers of rain in places dense with grief.
I am walking in ravines where drought has assembled the dead.

When god finally comes
and no one recognises her
I'll be out there walking

LEAVING

Parting

Finally, I wanted to say
watching you
like light in snow

Like straw in the beak
grain of wheat hooked in the claw

Like creases blue-black
between stars

Like apple's black seed
deep within its ventricle of flesh

Like moonstones
locked in underground chambers

Like planets flat-
packed in their paper latitudes

Like the act of parting
remarkable universe undoing itself

ELIZABETH CARRIERE

Old

The old one leans between the stones
pulling water from the creek
like a swallow drinking in flight.
Is he resting? All that age

slackening against the hungry earth.
He is still, he has time
to watch a sleeping worm
unclothe from her silken shroud.

He marks her resurrection
calculated against the social
calendar of bees. He counts
the moment when

the robin's embryo
locked in its cuticle of aqua blue
hatches under the faithful
clock of the full moon.

But he moves on
from the moon's keeping
rides the deep rivers of his veins
to open sea.

Beyond his skin. Beyond his country.
He does not find infinity. Only
the intimate sound of water
inside his body connecting

with a foreign ocean. His
bones open as a song.
His whole dear life converges, a
crust of light cresting on a single wave.

I Shall Be the Rain that Wants

You will find me
in all the wrong places
I shall be time

on your hands the flood
after the drought

I shall be the way
you look back and see

a black road with
no-one following

I shall be the journey
the leaving

the scenery descending
the ground giving

under you
a mirror smooth

as a calm day sailing
and after this

I shall be the wind
and the sharp crack

of freezing water the
way it drains away but

I am not the thin light
you walk on
as though it were solid ice

ELIZABETH CARRIERE

Michael

Because we see in each other
the birth of our deaths:
you say it is in my skin
the light fading from crystal
somewhere in my face
or hesitation in belief
or a slowness when I walk from
your anger

Because we see in each other
time making its way out of
places where we thought
we held it even the place
below your heart where I would
draw another heart has given up
its heat

Because we see in each other
bones behind these
masks of flesh the prudent artifice
in the way we summon
innocence into the rooms of
our gods

Because we see what
we no longer want to see
the line across the glass
and only the blue parts
of fire the windows closing
against darkening curtains
of trees

Because we do not see
the red promise
at either end of the day
the long-legged birds shadowed
against the sand in the same
way air rushed
toward the horizon
and away from evening
and out from green grasses
at the shore

Each of us has found
a new distance within this dream
memory scant as postcards
from those abundant journeys
this could be some strange alchemy
your heaven my earth
vaulting in the tempest
of this parting

ELIZABETH CARRIERE

Like Music

1.
In the city a small bird fights its neighbour
for a scrap of paper stained with grease

The arm of a stranger brushes yours
accidentally as you pass in the street

A channel of tainted water rushes out from
a cleft in the pavement opened by a green shoot

Above the mountain
the sun sets as a pink shadow

A train of lights appears in the night sky
arcs its way across and disappears into the tree line

A man holds his lover watching
the world as they know it collapse

2.
Away from the city a cricket pulses a shrill message
bats reel in the dark feasting

A tug thumps as it pulls a silent barge in the dark
its lights throb a bright path along the inlet

When you sleep your heart is full of poems
or when you sleep your heart is empty
you dream of sinking and loss

Around you night is a mantle
embroidered with fallen trees

You wake suddenly to staccato rainfall
sated animals skitter under the eaves

3.
At dawn the shrouded sun rises to birdsong
you gather all the noise in like children

Sounds break into chords
scatter into waves

They rush the shore like breaths
like music

ELIZABETH CARRIERE

As gods Do

The day ends as days end
with its hour of courage
its envelope of despair.

The mute mouse makes its peace
with a small space between the eaves.
The branches drop lustrous
portraits of summer just passed.

A plump bird, small as a butterfly, catapults
its soft body against bamboo shoots
to avoid the rain or a raven.

Even the water pulls back from the shrinking shoreline
Pulls, then surges against the pebbles -
cold and sure like death.

What is this grey air telling me?
It carries a message from you,
or from the god who steals light from the sky.

He is blameless in his grief,
as gods are when they destroy what
they have loved, as gods do.

Night

The night is able.
The night takes on the wind,
the murmuring swallows.
The night welcomes you as its star,
names your planet
by its angle to the moon.

The night is a fool.

The night was my right hand
and with it I drew a universe.
In it was a stone as smooth
and harmful as the aria's
top note, and as sad.

The night was my lover.

The night is a sleeve,
a glove clothing a gesture,
clothing all gestures. And
your mouth with its music,
your wrist with its intricate
arabesque.

The night took me in like
a mother. I was
night's child.
In that deepest dark
she calmed me.

ELIZABETH CARRIERE

The night becomes a sparrow,
a brown shadow that eats
its own dark,
folds its radiant wings,
dies in our russet
feast of dawn.

Again

The ache has found its way like rust
into the little pins that hold the day
like shirts on a line away from dust

You never meant I suppose to twist
truth to its darkest stain
indelible as words upon your tongue
repeated and as meaningless as pain

Oh I never meant to fall for that again

ELIZABETH CARRIERE

First

First the raven calls out a cry
that signals the sky's perimeter.
It reminds me of nothing.
I have nothing to forget:
a morning mercy.
The forests melt to snow
and heaven visits the vole
in her nest. The day begins
with this procession of lost
beginnings and small wonders.
Your hand on my shoulder.
Surely all the spirits keep
watch as the earth falls,
there in that one look.

Each

And those who are named
can they stay named?
They may be daughters too.
I rose thinking this.
Sound of water shaping
itself around the shore.
And raven's long wingbeats,
its call stopping short
an aviary chatting in the trees.
That was when I wondered—
my mind settling on the discomfort
of your memory—
about the name of each bird
and the name of each child.
Her history
kept in place by each upright
spear of grass, by each dream
at dawn.
Thunder in the wings
of each hummingbird.

ELIZABETH CARRIERE

Half-light

Before the rich unwarming of the sun
as dusk backs away from the day
when a swallow leaves its circling path
and dives between the steepled upper
branches of the pine

You lie outside on the daybed in the dwindling light
still recovering your body scorched earth
irradiated healing straps you to the coming days
your bones electric and porous

You make an arc with your arm dividing
yourself from brightness it is too much
the stippled moon looms white
at the edge of day where trees converge
slight swish of wind as the air cools and climbs
above the ridge

Below us the ferry rushes the dock
small boats rise in its wake
just as the sun rounds the last
cloud a sudden shard of light
lasers our silence
death peels away as though
it were a game for nightfall

At the house the fire we make
takes red breaths
the yard's rodents mutter in their nests
and grass lets out its damp scent
we wait for our guests
they will bring wine and flowers
and we will join hands again
in the half-light

Benediction

Who has named and numbered the steps to grace
Who has called out forms that shaped wonder

Who can call up the sounds of the earth
the sound of a feather stirring in a pool of grass

I am asking for a friend an animal or the dead
I am asking for all three because I know them all

They call me as I rest in that place between sleep and wakefulness
in those places between time and death and joy

Is there a time beyond now when this no longer matters
a time when the raven's call is the song I sing when I dream

A time when water creatures walk towards us on their knuckled fins
and speak their fishy words like the pearls they hold inside their bodies

I want this time but is it time to stop wanting
I catch my breath and it is a cloud of seeds a cloud of vapour

It is the sound a wolf makes in the bones of its throat
it is the whale's song strung like thread through molecules of ocean

It is not meant for me
it is the sound of benediction all the same

ELIZABETH CARRIERE

Girl

Leaf starched and yellow
freed from its limb falls
in argument with the wind
the tree lightens a little
from that simple parting

Stretch out your arm like that
holding an apple against the gold
evening sky
full of tomorrow's snow
a simple beauty
links two seasons one rich
and sweet what we
summon as memory
the swallow with her mysteries
the winter truths that sleep like birds
inside these hollows of frozen ground

Tomorrow is the season we won't imagine
caves filled with soot and scripture
forests deep with their own purpose
there! a girl moves into the green dark
vanishing and appearing
visible as a lantern between trees
unfixed, alone, hunting.

ABOUT THE AUTHOR

As an emerging writer, Elizabeth Carriere was immersed in the vibrant Saskatchewan writers' and broader arts communities. She was influenced by the creativity and activism of those communities, and her association with Canadian writers and artists generally. She was especially inspired by the leadership and imagination of her mother, Anne Szumigalski, to whom this volume is dedicated. When Carriere moved to Winnipeg, she became active in the Manitoba writing and arts community, and helped organize the Winnipeg Writers' Workshop, pushing for stronger recognition of Manitoba writers. Together with colleagues, she was co-founder of *Writers' News Manitoba*, which later developed into Prairie Fire. She participated in readings and events and had poems published in literary magazines such as *Grain, Writers' News Manitoba, and CVII*.

Carriere worked in Manitoba and British Columbia as a senior government official, and later as a senior diplomat in charge of development programs in South and South East Asia, the Caribbean, and Africa, for which she was awarded the OBE. She concluded her more than two decades overseas as Governor of the Caribbean Overseas Territory of Montserrat, and finally as Senior Regional Manager Central and East Africa with Care International, based in Rwanda.

She lives on Gambier Island, British Columbia.

Printed in Canada